One Good Turn

Poetry by
Kirston Koths

BLUE LIGHT PRESS ❖ 1ST WORLD PUBLISHING

1ST WORLD
PUBLISHING

SAN FRANCISCO ❖ FAIRFIELD ❖ DELHI

*WINNER OF THE **2016** BLUE LIGHT BOOK AWARD*
One Good Turn
Copyright ©2016 by Kirston Koths

1ST WORLD LIBRARY
PO Box 2211
Fairfield, IA 52556
www.1stworldpublishing.com
Email: worldlibrary@lisco.com

BLUE LIGHT PRESS
www.bluelightpress.com
Email: bluelightpress@aol.com

BOOK & COVER DESIGN
Melanie Gendron
www.melaniegendron.com

COVER ART (TURF SERIES #4)
AND INTERIOR ILLUSTRATIONS
Gwen Koths
www. koths.com

AUTHOR'S PHOTO
Riggy Rackin
www. riggy.com

FIRST EDITION

Library of Congress Control Number: 2016950317

ISBN 9781421837611

ACKNOWLEDGMENTS

Some poems in this collection have appeared in the following poetry publications:

Askew Poetry Journal: The Stud
California Quarterly: Snow Reader
Common Ground Review: The Davy Crockett Outfit
Echoes From the Heart (M Coffee Anthology): Letter From Havana
LILIPOH: King of the Cab
LIPS Poetry Magazine: Fight Night
Marin Poetry Center Anthology, Trees, Vol. XVI: Four Seasons of the Sugar Maple
Plainsongs: Double Swings
River of Earth and Sky: Poems for the 21st Century (Blue Light Press): Mrs. Perkins' Favor, The Force That Holds the Helix, An Irretrievable Sound, Snow Reader, Fight Night, King of the Cab, Letter From Havana, The Soul of Snowflakes

I thank many of the members of the thriving San Francisco Bay Area poetry community for their encouragement, mentoring, classes, and teaching-by-example, especially: Diane Frank, Ellaraine Lockie, Connie Post, Tom Centolella, and John Rowe.

I also am indebted to participants in the long-running Poets Across the Bay Workshop, particularly: co-founder Scott Caputo, Jeremiah Loverich, John Doiron III, Maggie Morley, Patrice Haan, Fred Ulrich, and Priscilla Wathington. And finally, I greatly appreciate the valuable input from my manuscript readers: Scott Caputo, Patrice Haan, and Diane Frank.

CONTENTS

THROUGH THE EYES OF CHILDREN

VOICES FROM THE JOURNEY

CALLED BY NATURE

TONGUE-IN-CHEEK

THE STORY WITHIN THE STORY

FRIENDS & LOVERS

THROUGH THE EYES OF CHILDREN

A child said What is the grass?
fetching it to me with full hands.

—Walt Whitman, *Leaves of Grass*

Fight Night

Friday evening was "Fight Night," back in 1954.
The Golden Age of Boxing had met the Miracle of Television,
and my parents' new set brought the neighbors to our house
like kids to a carnival.

Their fourteen-inch world of hazy black-and-white
came laced with ads for men's grooming and razors —
Brylcreem, a little dab'll do ya,
they'll love to run their fingers through your hair!

In Pittsburgh, boxing was king of all sports,
a daring distraction for the jaded rich,
pure inspiration for the poor.
Watching some "nobody" become famous for his fists
was a transparent drama with dark expectations —
controlled violence, a tonic for the tired
at the end of a steelworker's week.
Not a program for kids, said my mother.

Sent to bed early, one thin wall away,
I felt sleep come slowly in the acrid air
of unfiltered Camels and Lucky Strikes,
the announcer's voice almost singing
to the clang of the eager bell,
while men opened beers, yelled with each wild swing,
and women turned the crank on the chattering tub
of homemade, fresh peach ice cream.
We'll wake you up when it's finished, they promised.

In the quiet of next morning, I asked my parents at breakfast
why people lit cigarettes if the smoke stung my eyes,
why everyone cheered when the Negro got hurt,
why no one woke me for ice cream.

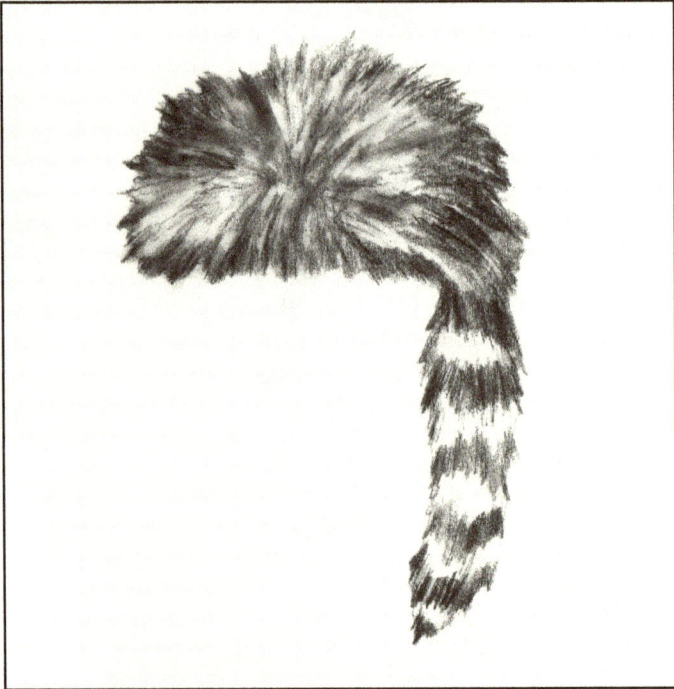

The Davy Crockett Outfit

The hat. I loved the hat.
In fact, his whole rugged outfit
was a parental bribe
that a feisty five-year-old could not resist.

Just behave for a week, and the next piece was mine:
the moccasins, deerskin leggings, the rubber Bowie Knife,
an air-rifle that shot a cool cork on a string,
and the coonskin cap with a tail that looked alive.

It was all just a game of see-sawing control
that ended as soon as my outfit was earned,
making me "King of the Wild Frontier,"
free once again to act up and annoy.

I had learned it from Tommy,
who didn't have a mom.
He did it, he said, to get back at his father,
that is, until his dad thrashed him hard.

Not with a belt, but a long buggy whip,
that lined his backside with red next to red.
Tommy told me the main thing it taught him
was how not to cry when it hurt.

That afternoon, as his ex-Marine father
slept off the stink of morning whiskey,
he showed me the welts and even the whip
that hung near his bed in their trailer.

I decided right then to be a good kid,
and my parents never figured out why.
Later, when they asked me what happened to my hat,
I told them I had given it to Tommy.
And I had.

Mrs. Perkins' Favor

Why is it now that I remember
four years old so much more clearly
than twenty-four or forty-eight?
As a boy of four you just need a floor
and a shiny train to play with
to create a world that you control
as the engine speeds and crashes.

But the comfort smell of oven cookies
is a full-fledged pheromone
of chocolate-sugar-butter-spice
to tiny noses such as mine.
Are those for us?

Remember Mrs. Perkins,
who lives one house down, across the street?
These are her favor, mom explains,
as she wraps them in waxed paper.
What's a favor? I need to know,
disappointed, but curious.
Something special you give a friend.
Her answer made me think.

"Favor" was a splendid word,
one I never have forgotten,
but also never heard again
in quite that wonderful way.
Perhaps my mother made it up —
she liked to make up words.

In any case, it now seems lost
from even the lyrical Midwestern lexicon.

I asked her when we would be going.
She said, *Oh, you can take it by yourself.*
You know the house. Just look both ways
before you cross the street.
Her voice was confident, assuring,
although I'd never been away from home before
alone. I swallowed slowly, and said, *O-kay,*
as the word stretched thin
somewhere between excitement and concern.

We had walked to Mrs. Perkins' house
on many other visits,
holding hands, a mother-son sweet snapshot
waiting to be framed.
But everything looked different now,
much larger and alive —
down the too-high, foot-smooth, stone front steps
between the angry, lion-headed pillars,
then past daddy's old Model A Ford
sleeping under streetside elms
with its springy, bouncy backseat.
No time now to watch the curving stream of ants
flowing from the sidewalk crack.
I had important things to do
with Mrs. Perkins' favor.

Held in my best both-hands grip,
it warmed my palms just slightly,
like mittens dried upon the hearth
before a winter fire.

A cookie peeked between the folds
beneath the truck-red ribbon.
If one somehow got "lost" upon the trip,
I wondered, would I be forgiven?

I almost crossed before I looked,
first one way, then the other.
The street swept out before me
like a field of head-high grass,
and once across, I looked right back
to see exactly what it was I'd conquered.

At Mrs. Perkins' doorstep now
a tiptoe stretch to reach the bell
brought her quickly to the screen door,
looking with large eyes
to find that I was there alone.
What have we here, my dear? she asked.
I said, *It's just your favor.*
The smile that spread across her face
was the biggest I'd seen,
ever.

On my way home I felt so proud
of making someone happy,
I crossed the street in half the time
and sang "Pop Goes the Weasel."
As I climbed back up the steps
that led up to our door,
in the big front window of our home
I thought I saw
the soft face of my mother
in between the curtains.

Ode to No. 2

Sometime after I had explored
the endless colors of Crayola 64,
but well before I could afford
the golden gleam of Cross
or fat-cat Mont Blanc ebony,
I seriously fell for you.

Who can forget those turned-on times
of dark, mechanical whirling rides
that left me holding you with pride,
and you in dizzy, sharp delight!

I wrapped you up so tightly
you made rose-colored patches on my skin.
Then I, with nervous nibbles,
left my own small marks behind
in purely primal mouthings.

How surprised you must have been
to see the passion fade,
my fascination whittled down.
Yet, when I finally knew for sure
your days with me were growing short,
I held you much more closely at the end.
Who stole my youthful love for you,
my school-bus-yellow pencil friend?

King of the Cab

Before my first day at Prairie Elementary,
my father enrolled me in a class of his own,
as he pulled me up, to work next to him,
in the rattling cab of his old Dodge dump truck.

Dad said the cracks in the sun-baked leather seat
looked a lot like a Midwestern map.
He asked me to follow along those little squares
with his prized Parker pen and its stream of bright blue,
to trace out our route just in case
we somehow got lost coming home:
turn right at the T, past Saddlebag Lake,
then two more lefts to the Lazy Bar R.

At each stop he loaded slop from the stockyard,
its head-turning stench an unmistakable mixture
of sweet hay, ammonia, and dark musty wet.
Great-looking food for the crops, he would shout,
but it's a darn good thing our fields don't have noses!

Dad told me our truck was pulled by horses
that lived up under the hood
and obeyed the grinding commands from a stick
that he helped me to shift through big H's and L's.
I looked down a hole in the rusted-out floor —
never did see any hooves.
And when no one was coming,
dad drove right down the middle
so I could watch the white dashes flash by.

The sun slumped to orange before we reached home,
where my father could harvest a sleepy-eyed son,
carrying me to the kitchen like a sheaf of spring wheat.
No matter that the eyelets of my dad's worn work shoes
were packed with manure from pigs and cows,
to me, he was King of the Cab,
tour guide to the gates of my beckoning new world.

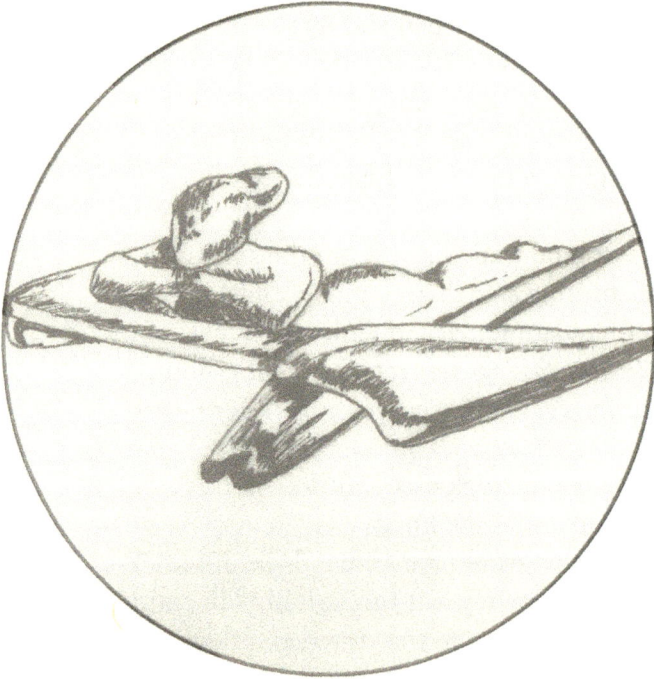

1955 Nash Rambler

They wanted one that said *the world war is really over* —
a car they could cruise in, down the new Interstate.
It's great for a family with two handsome young kids,
said the salesman in his tweed, double-breasted suit.
His forehead glistened like a greased hard-boiled egg
in the summer Indiana sun.

He talked a lot without listening, but Dad didn't care.
She's got the power to pull an Airstream trailer,
and you're gonna love those elegant curved lines!
Mom whispered that it looked like an overturned bathtub,
but to me that didn't seem so bad.
Not black, he droned on. *She's a two-tone, lime-white.*
Exactly the colors of Mom's Cottage Cheese Lime Jello Delight.

Dad liked the newfangled, reclining front seats
for those frustrating "No Vacancy" nights.
And the back seat had an armrest right in the middle
to keep my little sister off my side.
The spare's on the back in our new Continental Kit,
and the turning signals are optional, only 16 bucks.
Here's the key. Let's take her right out for a spin.

Mom loved the quiet ride of the white sidewall tires,
so Dad drove it faster, but the rattles were gone.
The car breathed fresh air through its big oval grille,
and the hood had an ornament of a daring nude woman
lying, face down, on a wind-swept wing.

Dad and the salesman took a short walk to talk,
man-to-man about money, I guess,
and when they came back, *We'll take it,* Dad said,
squeezing Mom with a tight, one-armed hug.
My sister and I jumped up and down, cheered,
and I ran over to touch the hood lady.

Eighteen hundred and twenty-five dollars,
plus sixteen more for the signals,
meant Spam at dinner for much of that year.
Not enough spare money to even go to the movies,
but 27 cents for a gallon of gas
bought the family an escape from our city apartment
to the cool countryside, where the Rambler would slow
so my parents could look at big houses and dream.

Dad prized that car, and he nearly polished the paint off it,
his free ride to wherever the road went.
One day I overheard the old man next door
say it was nothing but a wannabe Buick.
So your new car's a Rambler? he sneered across the fence.
No, it stays on the road pretty well, Dad smiled back.

And it did, until a camper trailer bent down the frame,
so badly that the rear doors wouldn't close.
Dad put us in the back, then ran rope underneath,
up through the handles to the top, like a noose.
And he bought each one of us a huge Banana Split
on the Sunday he sold it for lime-green scrap.

Double Swings

Dad bought our old house for its prized double swings
and had a picture from *Sunset* to prove it —
two swings on one branch of a towering acacia,
every kid's backyard dream.

No more schoolyard, chain-and-metal A-frames!
This right angle branch, as thick as most trees,
held side-by-side swings on long manila ropes
that smelled of life, like ship's rigging.

Each human pendulum was in it for the arc,
propelled by the innate physics of children —
leaning forward and back, the pivoting of calves.
Up and down, again and again.

The rush toward the ground,
the heart-pumping pause
at the top of the world, a new view of the yard
in the impossible freedom of sky.

Mother and Dad were proud of their swing trick:
wing-buddy flight, just like the Blue Angels,
alwaysperfectlytogether,
without holding hands.

The year Mother passed, the arborist came,
shortened the branch to lessen the weight,
and finally removed one whole swing.
The double was gone like a sunset, too soon.
Dad talked about selling the house.

Tonight, clear and windless, the termites are flying,
as they leave their thin feast of soft heartwood.
The acacia will fall, and we all will take wing,
no reason to arc,
no need for the swings.

VOICES FROM THE JOURNEY

Twenty years from now you will be more disappointed by the things that you didn't do than by the ones you did. So throw off the bowlines. Sail away from the safe harbor.

—Mark Twain

Eripitur persona, manet res.
(The mask is torn off, while the reality remains)

—Lucretius, *De Rerum Natura*

Letter from Havana

(August 13, 2003)

They're celebrating Fidel's 77th birthday
at a government ceremony where the riflemen aren't smiling,
but children with short memories are giggling in a circle
by the statue of Elian Gonzalez,
returned to his father's arms.

All the billboards still pretend
with the same propaganda,
flattering us with dry declarations
as disappointing as a rumless daiquiri.
Nothing is pictured that you can hold in your hand.

On the outskirts of this crumbling Mafia playground,
the skeptical village-square clocks
are once again ticking their talk of Revolution,
counting the days until the old man will die.

Tired of waiting, we've traded all that we own
for one last chance to be with you in Miami.
Over a barrel or in one, what's the difference?
sighs the lawyer driving our cab
to the broken-down boat.
There is no meter running on his angry monologue.

Even Hemingway, writing *The Old Man and the Sea*
in his book-paneled home outside of Havana,
reminded us all before he took his own life,
All good stories always end in death.

With our castaway crew of Castro's infidels,
we are finally no longer afraid of the ending,
of hauling up our anchor in the shroud of a dark night
and floating up to heaven,
in either direction,
just ninety miles away.

Desafortunado

Our tilting trail into the deep Copper Canyon,
awash last week with a warm silty flood,
is now a muddy track of tortilla chips,
baking in the Sierra Madre sun.
The empty melon bellies of our Tarahumara children
are crying like crows
for a meal of something more than last year's moldy corn.
The summer rains came late this year,
so the budding kernels barely grew.
When the showers came at last,
they washed the rest away.

But children still play on the canyon rim
like skinny dogs with happy eyes.
For tonight the shaman comes again
to suck white worms
from the stubborn gash on father's back
with a healing cornstalk straw
and to chew peyote around the fire
while he dances our death away.

By the cooling waters of the year-round spring
at the canyon floor Cantina,
the starch-shirted government agency men
are as smug as old Spaniards,
eating slices of fresh tangerine
while they subsidize our tribe.
A line of mute men, we wait for the clerk
to cash out our small welfare checks,

dressed to go hunting for some self-esteem
in our one set of city-fit clothes.
We soon lose it all to the tug of tequila,
the lure of Tecate and lime.

The bar closes at five, too early
to walk home drunk without any word
of new work or even fresh food.
In the shadow of the lone palm tree trunk,
we squat in a line, straight out from the base,
like an hour hand of fallen faces
moving only enough to keep up with the shade.

On the road to the Lost Spanish Cathedral
the young blonde backpacker, sightseeing alone,
never noticed the dark eyes dissecting her form
as she passed by the Cantina palm
or the slurred, foul whispers of three Tarahumara,
the same young men whose ancient mothers
had been raped by Conquistadors,
the shame of that cultural pollution by force
still seething in the stories of their grandfathers.

The response to that sorry seed is now sown again,
and we wonder what the government will do.
A paragraph in the nearest town newspaper recounts
her experience behind the crumbling cathedral
as another "incidente desafortunado,"
simply an unfortunate incident.

La Calle

When the sun goes down in small Mexican towns,
people are drawn to the street.
La calle provides their free entertainment,
and the *taberna* accordion revives all who hear
its confident message calling into the night.

La calle in the moonlit countryside
echoes with *holas* of stooped men meeting,
takes pride in the committed kiss of teen lovers,
anticipates in sly delight
the bump and rattle of each rusty truck.

Near the old city *centro*, *la calle* is narrow,
a cobbling together of past plans and new.
It funnels its travellers out into the *plaza,*
where couples stroll nightly the square promenade,
revolving together through the hot evening hours.

Others, who have left the thin tin of home,
are content just to watch the rotating show,
folded onto stairways or angled against walls,
walls that lean in as if straining, themselves,
to be closer to the gift of the street.

Atoll Farewell

A fisherman from the Big Island
told us the icecaps are melting.
I cannot see them. I only know
that salt from the rising sea
has poisoned our atoll's palms,
stunting the sweet coconuts
we harvest and trade for food.

Here, I stand on the speck of land
my grandfather settled forever ago,
now nowhere more than one worried meter
above the sea's high tide.
Today, the ocean sends us gentle waves
on a windless Polynesian day,
but soon it will spin out another angry typhoon,
push the tide across our reef,
and wash the last of our nervous huts away.

Where frigate birds and albatross
used to stop, they now fly on.
But the fish don't care.
They do not cling to this piece of sand.
They swim where they will, still dodging each day
the fall of my stone-ringed net

Our outriggers are loaded and ready,
the Big Island an all-day paddle
into the eastern dawn,
far from where the evening sun
sizzles back into the sea.

The Cavalry, Victorious, Returns to Reims

The Rhone flows by, unruffled,
as we spur for home at last,
past tangled rows of forgotten vines,
withered by the war.
Our weary steeds revive their prance,
as one by one they recognize the road.

When the cobble cloppings stop
to echo in the great cathedral square at Reims,
I am the first to top the stairs,
bareheaded for a silent prayer.

Then, dashing down the hidden steps,
I reach the vaulted chalk-walled rooms,
carved by ancient Roman vintners,
now filled with fine champagne.

You've waited all this time
for me to free with swing of sword
the wires that corked your passion,
now flying to the stars.

I hoist you up for all to see
your creamy mousse flow proudly down my hand,
then pull you to my lips to share
exactly how it feels to win.

Millennium New Year's Eve in Brazil

On the midnight beach in Rio
I imagine she is out there somewhere,
waiting to satisfy my collegiate craving
for the ultimate Millennium date.

Through a jet-lagged haze, I watch
the world's largest party unfold —
a swaggering shore filled with three million people
all smartly dressed in traditional white
for Carnival dancing in miles of soft sand
on the last night of its kind.

With white carnations and gladiolas,
we fashion our circular shrines
around holes filled with candles
sheltered from the soft evening wind.

Then making a wish for the newest New Year,
we must jump seven waves
and toss our flowers
as far out to sea as we can.
There's a cheer as a brief offshore breeze
takes them out to Yemanja, Goddess of Oceans
and approver of every new dream.

Away, down the beach, a gathering tide
of Brazil's proud national anthem
picks me up in its swell,
and I join with full voice
in out-of-synch mimicry.

Carrying her sandals and three white roses,
she impresses her way though the crowd.
Behind her, like snowy male egrets,
we are suddenly frozen mid-hunt,
captured ourselves, by a product of perfection
in the World's Capital of Cosmetic Surgery.

She reaches the water and flirts with the waves,
collagen-filled lips poised permanently for love,
breasts hovering magically, ready to land
like doves into gentle hands.

I lose my last chance to ask for a dance
as her samba shoulders zigzag
up the beach toward home.
Before I can follow, the world explodes.
Fire-falls of liquid comets
drip from the roof of the Copacabana,
and bouquets spangle the waiting sky
like a hillside of night-blooming cactus.

When it's all over,
the wind smells of burnt joy,
and a single white rose drifts silently
past the drunken young men
singing songs in Portuguese
and peeing into the dark warm sea.

On a Trip to Buenos Aires

Across the ballroom, my *cabaceo*[1]
flashes the message, *Come tango with me!*
Your Argentine eyes answer, *Sí,* with a nod,
and we meet as strangers,
torso pressed to torso on the crowded floor,
our faces close in concentration,
your breath a comfort in my ear.

We will dance this street dance of the *barrio* sailors —
slender men born *peso*-poor, but *estancia*-rich
for the moments they impressed the prostitutes of Buenos Aires.
Give in to me briefly, mystery woman,
and I will present you as The Most Beautiful One,
revealing your portrait to all who will watch
as we paint from the palette of our movements.

Your delicate hand, a teacup of caresses,
settles soft on the nape of my neck.
In close embrace, our legs stretch behind us,
like a living Eiffel Tower
that is poised to tango all night long
beside the sleeping Seine.

The passionate music empowers us
as we mirror the melodic drama
in the reedy strength of the *bandoneon*
and the brooding violins.
Our dance moves up from the floor,
feet balanced on an unseen axis,
gliding without any ice.

Through the slimmest of openings I leave between us,
you slip so boldly away,
daring me to enter the space that you claim
with the deliberate, slow sweep of your endless leg.
Together again for a moment, you tempt me
with a stream of sinuous, backward *ochos*
that curve from your shoulders, through hips and heels,
to the slender shoes that jewel your feet.

Too soon the flawless dance is done.
We hold our embrace past the last note's farewell,
like two married, old *tangueros*.
With no words exchanged, just telltale smiles,
we return to our separate tables,
already immersed in the memory.

cabaceo[1]: an Argentine custom for arranging dance partners, using discrete eye signals.

CALLED BY NATURE

"...in Wildness is the preservation of the world."
—Henry David Thoreau, *Walking*

The simple News that Nature told —
With tender Majesty.
—Emily Dickinson, *Number 441*

Like a Jaguar

(for Manuel Chac)

The Mayan fisherman balances broad shoulders
on legs that seem small for the task,
like a jaguar prowling the jungle's thick edge.
He poles his small *panga* along the Yucatan bay,
for once again, the tourists want to go fishing.

His russet face scans the shallow cove
for fish that to him are like jade.
I ask him why he does this, day after day,
and he says through his smile,
The sea, she is always good, my friend.
Bad things only happen on the land.

Nothing escapes his practiced eyes
that peer though skinny water
into swirls of turtle grass.
The bay, aqua and alive, tempts us in all directions.
Flat-faced Snook and Cubera Snapper
are caught, held close, mostly released.
Only keep what you need. It's the Mayan way.

He tells me some young men have given up fishing
to sell guns and drugs in the cities up north.
Even the ocean knows something is wrong,
sends in hurricanes to slow the cartels,
slaps their arrogant seaside hideouts,
filling the ground floors with sand.

What will he do when his eyes lose their edge?
I don't want to be a rich man, he says with a shrug,
just enough to buy a bit of my jungle.
There, he will live out his last days alone,
where summer thunder beats like an old Mayan drum,
and the coughing cry of the jaguar
celebrates its lonely dark hunt.

Four Seasons of the Sugar Maple

Winter's first thaw is sugaring time,
when Patuxet Indians taught the Pilgrims
to tap the spirit of maple trees,
collecting nectar from the sunlit side
through hollow fingers of sumac spigots
into buckets of dried birch bark.

Spring's warm dawn tells waking buds
to feather out the wooden wings
that try to fly but never will,
content instead to shelter
wood thrush, warbler, and scarlet tanager
in the cozy cloak of an emerald canopy.

Summer's heat stirs the helicopter seeds
to stretch their two wings wide,
waiting for a September breeze
to carry them, dizzy,
arm-in-arm,
to the fertile humus of the forest floor.

Fall's orange and red igneous array
is scattered by fisticuffs of wind-blown branches
slowly denuded to reveal
the thin blue skin of a chilly sky,
as the handprints of leaf upon liberated leaf
push back into the earth.

The Path That Is Made by the Water

Hear the wild river's clarion call —
a descant of trickling water bells
above the foamy riffle's drone,
urging us to join in its journey to the sea.
As I step downstream with my wading stick,
fly-fishing the cobbled river,
I leave no print of where I've been,
for my path is made by the water.

Come drift in my wooden McKenzie boat,
down through the canyon, where the rapids star.
See how it spoons with the crescent waves,
its curved keel rising into pointed ends
like the corners of a satisfied smile.
Feel the forward slide and the backward lean
with each pull and push of the oars,
as strong arms add just a tailoring touch
to our endless, slow-motion fall.
We survive the sharp rocks because the current shares
its deepest path through the water.

We'll rest our boat in the boulder's lee,
where the gentle eddy turns
and the steelhead stack as they head upstream
to cycle their lives again.
Will they choose to kiss our hand-tied flies
of silky blue and bucktail
and refresh our hearts with their sea-run strength
before we set them free?

These noble fish know a subtle truth,
that the river goes both ways,
and they follow the scent of their silvery first year
up the path
made by the water.

A Cricket in the House

Master of the corner concerto,
you make your leggy entrance self-assured,
ready to perform
in head-to-toe tuxedo black
complete with satin trim.

Scarcely heard through the hot afternoon,
like the piano player in a rowdy bar,
the rhythm of your tune keeps time
with each creeping red degree.

When the farmhouse work is done
and evening lamps are dimmed,
the hearth at last becomes your center stage.
But tonight there will be no thrown bouquets,
no backstage cupboard visits.

Your chirrup of cadenzas
brings up the lights, ushers in the broom
for a rough and rolling sweep outside.
The door clicks tight, and curtains are drawn,
for all that matters now is sleep.

Cape Cod, 1957

I'm coaxed into napping by the cycle of the surf,
then wake to the scent of our musty tent in the sun.
Pumped-up whispers from the two-burner Coleman
convince me that my parents' huge pot will soon boil.
My tight face twists away from the crimson cries
of three live lobsters, waving so briefly
to cooks who never even noticed.

In a pie-tin ocean, my hermit crab captives
compete for new homes amidst the empty shells.
Periwinkles open their single eyes underwater,
looking around for a friendly explanation,
while sand castles, like gray memories,
soften back into the shore.

Cloud Illusions

It's cloud illusions I recall. —Joni Mitchell

In the Shetland Isles, a mackerel sky
swims far above the North Sea wharf,
schools of silver gliding,
beyond the reach of trawler's net.

Cirrus clouds of Phoenix, dry as down,
hold tightly to their showers,
while Navajo farmers dance for rain
to drummers on high mesas.

Mount Fuji crafts its own close cloud,
the loyal kind that never moves,
a misty monocle, where one end forms
as the other leaves, reluctantly.

Dark cones dance on the Kansas plains.
The sirens wail a warning,
but TV crews deny the risk
and make some funnel famous.

In Kentucky's sky, three Mare's Tail clouds
drift high above the Derby track.
Not a jockey in sight, still the fillies finish —
win, place, and show.

The Soul of Snowflakes

Awakening from a diaphanous dream
in a purple sky of clean clear cold,
embryonic droplets fuse
in a prelude to a million births
somewhere near the hand of God.

Like circular stained glass windows
growing outward in angel white,
each star-trimmed filigree is formed
according to divine designs
of delightfully ordered randomness.

Cascades of cartwheeling fairies
and whirling discs of Da Vinci men
sift through unseen fingers,
sailing to uncertain fates below.

Some settle onto groves of Douglas fir,
where artists will paint them in the morning light.
Others, rudely blown by unkind winds,
smash luckless into harder lands,
breaking fingers, even losing limbs.

Another few spend their final moments
in curious Molly's tiny outstretched hand,
as she closely considers the beauty of each
to prove for herself
that no two are exactly alike.

But just as quickly as they were conceived,
the snowflakes twist back into tears,
then to swirling vapors
searching skyward once again
to find the dark celestial womb.

Snow Reader

Passage through the woodland
is remembered by the snow, the gentle kind
that falls like sifted flour
and allows no secret trespass.

Where ruffled grouse have gone,
there's story in their trident stride
through grasses bent with seed,
tracing circles in the snow.

The seated fox leaves a melted round
that held sly patience in the dusk,
as henhouse chickens entered sleep,
heads tempting like warm biscuits.

The flap of owl wingtips
frames a furrow in the white,
quotation marks around
the muffled cry of mouse.

My footprints, much the coarser,
needing less than stealth,
track my morning progress
through the wintry pages.

Hurry now. The frozen record fades,
soft and wider in the bright of day.
All too soon,
no one else can know.

TONGUE-IN-CHEEK

If this is coffee, please bring me some tea;
but if this is tea, please bring me some coffee.

—Abraham Lincoln

Comic Relief

Life is not a comic book. Too bad.
KAPOW and *BONK* actually hurt.
Likewise, those chronic pains
that elicit *UUNH* and *OW.*
The anvil of old age lands hard,
with no hope for a Road Runner recovery.

I'd like to wear, like Daffy Duck,
the smoking feathers of exploded youth
and know that all will be restored
with a simple change of scene.

Please cast me in some bold cartoon
where the characters never age!
I'll vow to avoid all Kryptonite,
eat spinach by the can.

And when the real Grim Reaper comes,
I'll be ready when he does,
to bust his deadly scythe apart
with *THWACK* and *BIFF* and *BLAM.*

Knots

No, you can't wear your bedroom slippers,
said my mother, insisting that two well-tied sneakers
were suddenly my passport to playing outdoors.
You're old enough now to tie them yourself,
and I've written you a poem to help you learn how.

Make a little teepee and go inside with the chief.
Pull it up tight and then make a leaf.
Go around the stem, but keep it wide,
And push another leaf to the other side.
Then pull on both leaves and make them grow.
That's one shoe done, one more to go!

My struggle to solve this necessary unfairness,
hunched over on the cold hallway floor,
convinced me completely of the value of poetry,
more than any dozen teacher's tricks.

As for those knots, I never mastered them all:
the Windsor, the Bowline, the Clove Hitch, and Barrel,
the Fisherman's Clinch, the Trucker's Hitch,
the fundamental Monkey's Fist.

You can't call me a sailor, a camper, or a cowboy.
I never learned the ropes.
I'm a man still in love with Velcro and Bungees,
zippers, duct tape, and loafers.
And when it comes to tying, I depend on my friends
to save us all from the entropy of loose ends.

Farewell to Wisdom

They're like tailbones growing in the back of your mouth — vestigial,
my dentist droned on. *Pull 'em out!*
They haven't had a function since primitive man
started softening his food with fire!

Suppose, I protested, they're called "wisdom teeth" for a reason,
and if you yank them, you could damage my brain.
Superfluous teeth maybe, but retained, nonetheless.
There's a reason that Nature never works in a hurry,
and besides, they don't hurt. Let's leave them alone.

You can't keep them clean; they'll be nothing but trouble.
They're the Devil's teeth, and they really must go!!
I looked for the Tooth Fairy, but she'd been frightened away,
and my chipmonked mouth, stuffed with long cotton rolls,
was no match for this man,
who took my weak shrug for approval.

This won't hurt a bit, he lied, without blinking.
With senses now numbed by his Novocain trickery,
the Cro-Magnon part of my brain sent a signal,
giving my jaw the nerve to bite back.
Ouch, he cried, *How'd that happen?*

Only the edge of my clumsy tongue
seemed pleased to see them go,
the twisting tool held high
with another scarlet dentist's prize,
memories of crushing mastodon marrow
slowly slipping away.

Bad

I've been good my whole life,
and look what I've got —
an apartment so spotless it doesn't seem real,
and a husband who nightly never looks at my face.
That's why I want to be bad.

Maybe I'll use ashes for eye shadow
and a bit of my blood to color my cheeks,
staple a stud through my tongue at the mall
and lick any guy who thinks for a minute
that you can't conquer sad with some bad.

I'll defy my mother's tattoo taboo
with a punk purple spider on a shrunken black heart,
then bike through the Badlands with Hell's leathery Angels
to prove that there's nothing
much better than bad.

Ignore those new bills! I'll live the brash life
on my crumbling facade of good credit.
Toss out the cottage cheese. Bring me Red Bull and vodka!
No need to eat right
when you're running on bad.

Pick me! Pick me! I'm trying to be
the next bad apple of your eye.
I'll be laughing, of course,
and I'll show no remorse
for how badly I need to be bad.

Flower Competition on Prom Day

In the flower-shop cold room, petalled colors compete,
posing with confidence in tall metal cans,
eager to be chosen by uncertain young men
buying their first corsage.

The odds-on favorite to come in first,
the rose should win it by a nose.
These crimson couriers of passion's scent,
rule like queens on their slim green thrones.

Close behind, come the elegant orchids,
who pose aloof with open lips,
each one angling for an amorous eye,
so ready for a prom-night kiss.

White lilies are pure, but they're fast at the finish,
willing to shed their habit of innocence
in a moonlit field
with the captain of the football team.

Each bloom waits for the winner's reward —
a snip and a wrap of green florist's tape,
looped with elastic on a ready wrist
for one perfect night on the town.

This Poem Is Safe for Real Poets to Read

Because nowhere is there any mention
of the tired topics that tax your attention.

Nothing too religious or pompously pedantic,
or gory or sexist or hopelessly romantic.

No run-on rants in a page-long stanza,
not a single shape-poem extravaganza.

All enjambment will run like clock-
work with the language of Poe
-etry.

No annoyingly consonant sonic romances,
lackluster alliteration, only lines that take chances.

No worn clichés or dubious timing,
beating a dead horse or obvious rhyming.

The Poetry Police have the gerunds arrested,
and you won't be seeing adverbs, since they're *totally* detested.

There's not one line that's formulaic,
pornographic, trite, ARCHAIC.

Alas, what is left? I have to ask.
Following these rules — an impossible task.

In the end, it seems I've been caught in a lie.
I had good intentions. I really did try.

It's greeting-card verse, a long way from professional,
and now it's even turning confessional!

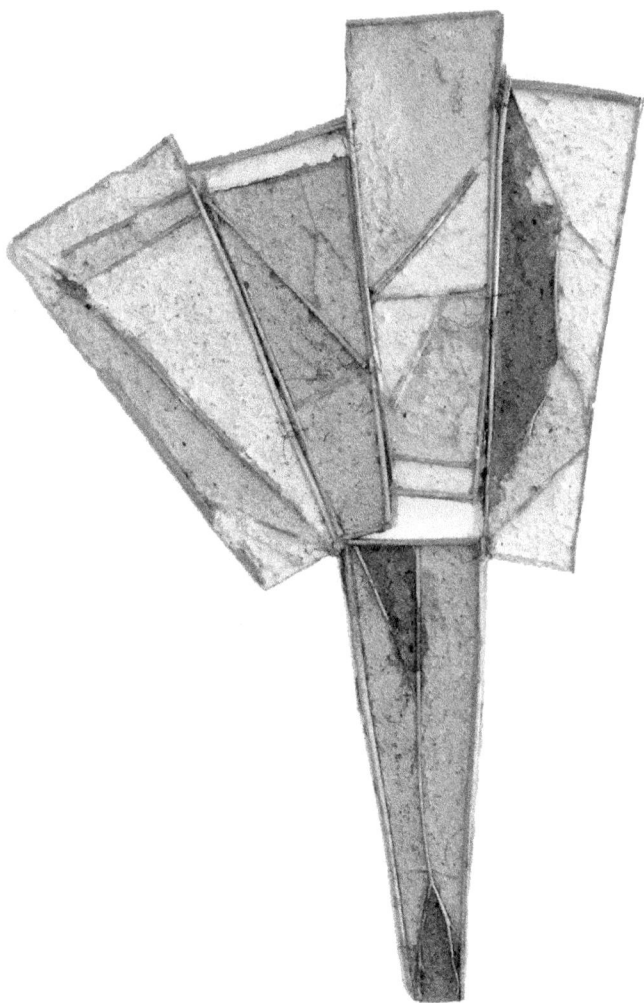

THE STORY WITHIN THE STORY

It was the best of times, it was the worst of times. . .
—Charles Dickens, *A Tale of Two Cities*

No change of circumstances can repair a defect of character.
—Ralph Waldo Emerson, *Essay III. Character*

The Stud

He worked his Wrigley's with his mouth wide open,
apparently a casualty of casual.
But the babes at the bar couldn't seem to get enough
of his Marlboro Man poses
and his muscular phrases —
Hey, I'm creaming to that!
Naw, I'm chucking to that,
the entire panoply of life's emotions
divided into just two macho extremes,
all by the age of twenty-five.

As the Reno showgirls glide in after work,
the cowboy polishes the tips of his boots
on the back of his dusty Levis,
then leans in to hear the gossip and worse
from their parallel universe.
Leveraging his looks, he places his bet
on the cute one who winked as she entered,
and soon he is leaving with his sweet slot machine,
her eyes rolling up like two matching cherries
just before the payoff.

Not Winning

Life is just high school with variations. —Anon.

Still living at home
ten years after high school,
Hey, you texted,
Wanna go 2 r Class Reunion?

Touchdown Tony, Rambo, V8,
all the guys showed up
to drink a few beers, re-live the good times.

V8 asked if we all remembered
the time I pinned you in just thirty seconds,
wrestling in gym class, while everyone watched.
You were bigger than me and one teen-year taller.

I did remember Coach yelling: *Takedown, two points.*
And then the smell of your callisthenic sweat
that smeared on my face as you tried to escape.

And the satisfying sound as Coach slapped the grey mat
three times.
Winning? I really don't recall, I said,
seeing the angle of your eye, the fall of your face,
so wrapped up in that lost moment.

Little League Umpire

I could have stayed home
to watch the Yankees play the Red Sox,
but I donated my day to be a Little League ump,
to savor the sounds of a hometown rivalry —
the ping of aluminum bats making contact,
the revved up cheers of support from the fans.

Half the crowd backed the boys from Al's Auto.
The rest were for Ace Sand and Gravel.
As I made my calls of balls and strikes,
a rattling voice stood out in the stands,
one dad's unmuffled opinion
each time his boy came to bat.

You kidding me?
That was waaay outside!
Get some glasses!

When his son hit a go-ahead longball in the fifth,
and the catcher tagged him out in a dusty collision,
this guy was in my face faster than an airbag,
with battery-acid accusations and cusses that leaked
past the gasket of his tightly pressed lips.

With that, he pulled his boy from the game,
pushed him, red-faced, into a matching Camero,
and peeled out of the parking lot,
the whiny sound of shifting
fading in the distance,
anger leaving, gear by gear.

No Stopping on the Bridge

In search of a different answer,
he walks onto the Golden Gate at dusk,
but finds no solace in the cable-drone
of harp strings that tremble
as they hold up the heavy road.

The face of The City shines in the distance,
so near you could almost reach it
in a single, confident stride.
Time heals all wounds, they always told us.
What time is it now? he wonders.

The signs all say
No Stopping on the Bridge.
Yet the four-foot railing,
more Deco than deterrent,
invites him to step to the other side.
He falls without a sound, a cold comet.

One by one, the curious gulls
shriek and leave their steely perches,
spiral down like draining dreams
to inspect the broken form,
another floating number
in the welcoming foam.

Too Late, They Noticed

How you bring your own gravity
when you arrive at a party,
expect galaxies of men to change their hot orbits,
and they do, curving in like meteorites.

One by one, you incinerate their gifts,
only to dawn later on some new suitor
who mistakes your incandescence for the sun.

They fly like hummingbirds to a nectarless sunflower,
sip from your empty lips, drop weak from the sky —
Icarus after Icarus.

Too late, they noticed
how you cycle through partners with each change of season,
drive your Sun Chariot, never stopping,
never looking back.

King Akhenaten

You, yourself, are lifetime. —King Akhenaten, *Hymn to the Sun*

Sun lights up his statue in the Museum of Cairo,
and he almost speaks, as he reigns tall and handsome
over a dingy side room with its faded display.
There, I learn how King Akhenaten,
the dark-skinned pharaoh,
ruled all of Egypt for seventeen years
yet lost his legacy so swiftly
that few would remember his name.

Akhenaten allowed worship of only one God, Aten —
the sun-spirit, always shown as a golden arc,
each ray ending in an outstretched hand.
The Pharoah alone could speak for Aten,
gutting the power of the old temple priests and their pantheon.
They watched in wary awe of their confident leader
and his thin-necked queen, Nefertiti,
who for sixteen years tried to bear him a King Son,
passing him only six daughters.

Was he murdered or was it an illness?
No one wrote it down
in the rush of joyous priests to dismantle his palaces
and chisel off all signs of Aten.
No grand pyramid, no gold-filled sarcophagus,
just Tomb 55 in the Valley of the Kings.
Only this stark stone likeness
and the now-famous bust of Queen Nefertiti
abandoned, unclaimed, on the sculptor's workbench
in the deserted city of Akhenaten.

Champlain's General Store

I remember Vermont in the 1960s,
with its train-station towns the Interstate had widowed,
its grandfather barns under folded tin hats,
and the curve of the river
past fieldstone skeletons of streamside mills
where water used to work.

Champlain's General Store was a major attraction
to my little sister and me —
a hanging museum of washboards,
bear traps, and two-handled saws,
and a banner on the wall that said *Live Free or Die!*

Late in the day, folks would stop by
to check in on old man Champlain
and freshen up their gossip around his wood-burning stove,
with no serious thought of spending very much
other than a bit of their time.
As he listened, he sucked on his unlit bone pipe
like a thirsty child at a bottle gone dry.
I suspect he heard poorly, if he heard much at all,
since he mostly said *Pardon me?* and *That's purdy nice.*

Old man Champlain was our hometown folk hero,
descended from the Revolutionary War's Green Mountain Boys.
After school, we all would hop on our Schwinns
with playing cards clothes-pinned onto the frames
so the spokes would sputter in bold staccato
that big motorcycle sound.

The faster we peddled our homemade Harleys,
the louder our paper engines roared.

Down to Champlain's, where twelve cents in your pocket
was a penny-candy party
of lollipops, licorice, Tootsie Rolls, and taffy,
Black Jack gum, and Atomic Red jawbreakers.
And for the kids with a grown-up swing in their stride
he had candy cigarettes and bubble gum cigars.

One hot afternoon, a biker gang from the city
bullied him again for money and beer,
but this time they hit him too hard.
When our parents found out,
they made each and every one of us
take the playing-card engines
off our imaginary motorcycles,
hoping somehow it might help.

Looking for America, 2001

Counting the cars on the New Jersey Turnpike,
They've all come to look for America. —Paul Simon, 1969

Their symbolism, for some, was easily ignored,
that is, until they were gone.
The soaring twin conduits of commerce
stood silent, like sentries
for a world made of money.

In the quiet sunrise of September,
the angry young men with no luggage
sliced sideways into our lives.
We tried to make sense of the horror and hate
but could not stop watching the replay.

We cried for the leaping few,
who never knew the crumbling.
Then we waited to hear from the firemen,
but they vanished into heroes in an instant.

Cloaked in the dust of death,
the survivors returned,
a wide-eyed mayor and anonymous men,
until the last truckloads of hope
had finally been hauled far away.

———

Possessed by a pilgrimage, carloads of tourists
arrive from the turnpike each day.
They drive toward a new, western Mecca,
past the "Have You Seen" posters of unsuspecting faces,
pictured in happier times.

In response to its unplanned attraction,
the City issues time-coded tickets
for thirty-minute viewings in scream-filled silence
from a platform of flowers and newly found flags.

Nothing unimportant ever happens in New York.
Maybe that's why we've all come to look,
to search for something other than emptiness
in the void of a fathomless hole.

Memories of an Iraq War Vet

Veterans account for about 10% of all U.S. adults.
—*Time Magazine*, July 23, 2012

When I ask once again about the War in Iraq,
you finally tell me the way it went down —
how they made you burn your questions
on the pyre of combat logic
and bury them along with enemy bodies in the sand.

You begin the story of their cowardly attack,
and I'm instantly struck
by the glaze of your ceramic stare,
fired in the flash of a roadside bomb.

In full battle gear, you shared their stony path,
no place for the shoeless,
where even the smallest cut
scabs but never heals.

You tell me of a daffodil dropped in a village lane,
its flower splashing like a broken egg.
How you saw snow fall in the desert.
Snow, in the desert, you say.

FRIENDS & LOVERS

The only way to have a friend is to be one.
—Ralph Waldo Emerson, *Essays: First Series*

"All You Need Is Love"
—John Lennon & Paul McCartney, *Magical Mystery Tour*

An Irretrievable Sound

The thin, white moon had arrived like an ambulance
to carry off the dying dusk.
A January rain fogged my windshield,
and the swift road turned darker than night.

Inside the warm car, it rained relaxation.
The reassuring sound of your calm conversation
and the sexy salve of blue radio jazz
made the highway exits coast by in a blur.

All at once, worried taillights
telescoped toward us,
a warning in bloody Morse Code.
I was still going sixty, distracted
by the drama of a roadside wreck,
until the time for any stopping had passed.
In your scream was the sound of life leaving
as I swerved sharply left into blackness.

We slowed in silence, in the left-hand lane,
while alternative endings played in high definition
on the wide screen of our startled senses.

I mumbled something flimsy about the crazy other car,
and flogged myself mentally for not paying attention.
You apologized for screaming,
but it didn't come close
to taking that sound away.

The Force That Holds the Helix

While the force that holds the helix wasn't watching,
some tiny hooded horsemen
slipped inside my cells
to rob me of a perfect wholeness.
Within those precious bosom cells,
the lusty focus of my lover's glance,
their dirty stable doubled daily
until the thriving roundup of clandestine death
was discovered by a touch.

The "Path Report" was cold, correct,
not much room for error.
Aggressive carcinoma of the breast,
I heard the careful surgeon say
through the earmuffs of my shock,
and I'm quite concerned about the mets.
Somehow, I knew he wasn't talking baseball,
but then I saw the scoreboard numbers
all rolling back to zero.
Metastases, I mean,
so we'll have to take the nodes as well.

In the soft light of the pre-op room,
the thoughtful nurses left us to ourselves
as the crucial question came.
Will you still love me
just the way you always have,
when I start winking at you
with my chest?

He heard the comic courage
weakly laughing, crying,
laughing, crying.
Of course I will, he hugged right back,
and I tightly held with hope
his trembling hands.

Amuse-Bouche

amuse-bouche: French term for a complimentary, unexpected bit
of food served before the meal arrives, often revealing the chef's
approach to the art of cooking.

You amuse my mouth every time we meet.
Not in the way that famous chefs
serve a miniscule capful of caviar on toast
and a dollop of tempting crème fraiche.
But with the warm promise of your willing lips
as they pout, then smile, in the subway car.

Anonymous traveler, who shares each day
my crowded commute to work,
how I've secretly hungered to know you.
Today, as we hold on side-by-side
for my one-stop ride, you whisper,
A soft kiss is the condiment of love.

The doors close behind me,
and I turn to see your air-kiss smile
through the accelerating window.

With our menu memorized,
we both know what we want,
everything imagined,
the mind already focused
on the virtual reality
of what comes next.

At the Pioneer Cemetery in Green Ravine

I've fallen from a shaken nest, you told me,
the time your father left for good.
We were up in Green Ravine,
two teens alone by the millpond,

when the crazy recluse, Farmer Green,
chased us off with a shotgun blast of rock salt.
I'll teach you young'uns a lesson,
he hollered from his truck.

Finally home from college, and twenty-something certain,
you say, *Let's go back to Green Ravine.*
We hike together toward an old frontier,
down a one-lane gravel road, our feet in dusty cadence.

The wrought-iron cemetery gate creaks free
for our short walk up the hill,
where buggies once bore proud pioneers
to lay loved ones beneath their story stone.

What calls us to this forgotten place?
What makes us lie down, so alive,
feed each other hunks of cheese,
sip wine straight from the bottle?

Your fingers hush my lips to hear
a tapping bird's percussive quest,
a hunt for hidden sustenance
so near the edge of all alone.

You play the petal-pulling game,
He loves me. He loves me not.
And when your hand finds room in mine,
our lives are wired electric.

Come get us, Farmer Green! I shout.
Your weightless arm curls around my waist,
and we cross the Great Divide, explore
the wilderness within us.

A Walk with Bella

To my golden retriever, the unfenced world is a beacon.
If the sun is low, and she's had no walk,
her patient sitting edges closer.
It happened like that today.
We rushed down our street to the nearby woods,
Bella tugging at the leash with an urgent agenda
that only another dog would understand.

For me, it's a walk. For her, it's much more —
as she samples the air in hurried sniffs
that analyze an aromatic zoo,
recording the origin of each signature scent.
She stops near the brush at the forest's edge,
right paw cocked in ready tremble
as her wet, black nose does its ancient job.
No danger lurks near the imaginary fire-circle,
no prey here worth pursuing.
We agree to amble on.

For some curious reason dogs prefer people
over life with another dog.
The pack is passé,
and the wariness of the wolf is long gone.
Bella's brown eyes lock straight onto mine
and ask me hard questions,
fantail waving in double-time
to the beat of a satisfied heart.

At the crosswalk light, I say, *Sit*,
but she looks quickly away,

in search of someone with a more amusing request.
As the light says *Walk*, a slow sitting begins,
an obedience that emerges like a gift from within.

Back home, in the den, she rests at my feet,
pants with a tongue of slant, dangling pink
and decides to offer her paw, our agreement
to hunt tomorrow again.

About the Author

KIRSTON KOTHS began collecting subject material for his poems when he was four years old, as a child in the Midwest. After a brief hiatus to get a PhD at Harvard and spend a few decades developing cancer biotherapies in the biotech industry, he finally returned to his lifelong passion, the arts. He currently does freelance writing, traditional music, studio recording, and documentary videography in the San Francisco Bay Area. Kirston knows that a new poem is finished when he can read it out loud and his golden retriever, Bella, does not leave the room.

Book Design, Artwork, and Photography

Cover Art and Interior Illustrations: GWEN KOTHS, a nationally renowned, prize-winning artist, is the sister of the author. After graduating from Cornell University, she established the Stone Turret Studio in Philadelphia, where she gives instruction in painting, juries art shows, and curates public art venues. Ms. Koths specializes in botanical watercolors and landscapes in oils.

Book & Cover Design: MELANIE GENDRON is an artist, author and book designer from California. She has done layout and design for over 100 books and chapbooks, including many that feature her distinctive artwork.

Photography: RIGGY RACKIN is a photographer and performer of traditional music, widely known for accompanying his singing with the English concertina.

www.ingramcontent.com/pod-product-compliance
Lightning Source LLC
Chambersburg PA
CBHW032027090426
42741CB00006B/758